Miss Twizzy

Lulu Gee

Miss Twizzy

Paperback

ISBN: 978-1496143037

Published by; Shoestring Book Publishing.

Copyright 2014
By, Lulu Gee
Illustrations by Peter King

Layout and design by Shoestring Book Publishing

For information address;
shoestringpublishing4u@gmail.com

Dedication & Acknowledgements:

For my grandson, Toby.

I would like to acknowledge Peter King for his wonderful artwork, he seemed to know instinctively how Miss Twizzy should be portrayed.

Also, my wonderful husband, the poet Daniel Lake, for his untiring patience, support and belief in Miss Twizzy from conception.

Miss Twizzy

Lulu Gee

Broomfield Farm...

*Miss Twizzy lives tucked in-between
the pig-sty and the barn,
behind the old worn-out machine
that long-ago spun yarn,
her door's painted in shades of green,
now peeling here and there,
so camouflaged and can't be seen
by portly cat's wild stare.*

*Miss Twizzy's neither young nor old,
she's also in-between,
yet finds an hour or two each day
to polish whiskers clean
and flick with feathers round the house,
when dust becomes knee-high,
and Tilly spider's upside-down
With hopes to catch a fly.*

*She sees each day old farmer Squidge
when scamp'ring through the yard,
zig-zagging ev'ry obstacle
when portly cat's off-guard -
asleep beneath the sycamore
he dreams of mack'rel fried,
and catching Twizzy long before
she has a chance to hide.*

New Curtains

Miss Twizzy's house with peeling paint,
with doors askew, some say, 'is quaint,'
Is tucked beneath the old farmhouse
just perfect for a little mouse.
With shutters painted in a shade
of scrumpy luscious marmalade
and windows of all size and shape,
so curtains hang, poorly agape.

Until that is her aunty May
brought needles, thread and with pince-nez,
sat high upon a bobbin reel
to stitch with haste scarlet chenille,
for Twizzy's curtains, that would drape
to fit her windows any shape,
with polkas dotted here and there
to match the cushion on the chair.

The sewing needle stitched so fast
Miss Twizzy held her head, aghast,
for in a week aunt May had sewn
with paws hard laboured to the bone,
new curtains in each size and shape
but now no longer hang agape.
and so at night 'til stroke of dawn,
Miss Twizzy's drapes are firmly drawn.

Miss Twizzy is Saved

Whoever would have thought to find an itsy bitsy mouse,
curled tight inside a coconut atop the sparrow's house.
She'd scampered with a hop and leap chased by the portly cat,
through cabbages and rows of bean she swerved this way and that,
Then passed a mallard duck who quacked shooing her ducklings on
while in the farmyard honking geese chased loudly Sissy swan.

Miss Twizzy searched for somewhere safe to rest a little while
and found herself by Lily lamb who had the sweetest smile.
So in the old barn Twizzy sat twitching her little paws
beneath the tractor, idle now and Percy Pig's loud snores.
Then suddenly the portly cat came thund'ring through the door
and with a cry each of them shook while Percy honked, 'guffaw.'

The day was cloudy, hazy blue with just a hint of breeze,
as to and fro the swallows flew with young amongst the trees.
And from the very tallest branch upon the tallest tree,
brown owl sat high with squinty eyes while watching Twizzy flee.
With squinting eyes he wasn't sure if she was here or there,
but took a chance to swoop her up, for dinner was now rare.

Now all this time the swallows had seen squinty owl drift low
and when they saw poor Twizzy caught just where the poppies blow,
they dealt a raucous, fierce fight against owl in midair
and with such wisdom owl had left, he dropped Miss Twizzy there.
High through the air Miss Twizzy flew to land on sparrow's house,
where apples and a coconut, awaited Twizzy mouse!

Twizzy's First Christmas

Miss Twizzy was on Christmas Eve sat by the pantry door,
to see the turkey stuffed with sage, grown wild with hellebore,
while farmer Squidge had chopped a spruce, so by mid afternoon
from every branch a bauble hung with ribbons to festoon.

And all the while the portly cat was dozing heavy-eyed,
with purrs louder than Christmas bells beside the fireside.
About the walls were Christmas cards with robins in the snow
and hanging from the chandelier, balloons and mistletoe.

Miss Twizzy ate warm pastry crumbs old Mr Squidge had dropped,
and portly cat jumped to the roof as champagne corks were popped,
while crackers with a glass of port were left for Santa Clause
and for the reindeers pulling him, some carrots placed outdoors.

'Twas when the house was fast asleep on this her first Christmas,
that Twizzy longed to stay awake, unlike the most of us -
so with much eagerness and yawns Miss Twizzy climbed the tree,
to sit beside the Fairy Queen, in crown and finery.

Then suddenly the Christmas tree shook wild her fir bodice,
as elves and soldiers came to life for this one night of bliss,
while trumpets blared the angels sang and soldiers with cymbals,
were marching fast as drumbeats rolled, dislodging pine needles!

For Twizzy mouse this was such fun, as gingerbread men danced
and silvery bells were tinkling as candy canes entranced,
while Twizzy clapped her paws with glee, enchanted by this sight,
awaiting Santa Clause to come, before dawn's early light.

The minutes on the Grandpa clock chimed loudly on each hour,
but weary now with tiredness Miss Twizzy lost willpower,
and fell asleep high in the tree beneath the mistletoe
and never saw dear Santa Clause, or heard him sigh, ' ho, ho.'

Scrumping ...

'Tis summer in the orchard and the perfect place to be,
for Twizzy loves it best of all beneath the apple tree.
She senses that the portly cat from his contented purr,
is dozing by the stable doors where breezes are astir.

So in the orchard Twizzy sits beyond where cattle feed,
just as the setting sun goes down and night comes guaranteed.
For high upon the twisting boughs the apples, shiny red
are teasing little Twizzy mouse who stands with paws outspread.

'Tis at the set of sun she knows there'll be a free for all,
for Willy wagtail with a smile will make the apples fall.
No longer hanging from the tree like a forgotten bell,
Miss Twizzy takes a joyful bite just where the apple fell.

Now Farmer Squidge has seen all this and portly cat has stirred,
but Twizzy just ignores them both while nibblin' undeterred,
Until that is old Farmer Squidge descends with urgent haste,
to throw at Twizzy an old boot as portly cat gives chase!

The air is blue as earthenware as Farmer Squidge cries loud
instructions to the portly cat, who scowls with ears bowed
at being woken to give chase through barns and fields of hay,
alas! He lost her in the coop to scrump another day!

The Cruise

As Twizzy rose one mournful day to heavy drops of rain,
beneath a sky of thund'ry cloud that spun the weather vane,
she thought of cousin Melody, who lived by Froggy's pond,
together with her aunty May, of whom she's very fond.

'Twas far beneath a stooping sky she scampered through the corn,
though stopping once, or was it twice to rest awhile and yawn,
while all the time the rain fell hard, louder than one drumbeat,
and suddenly she knew a flood was threatening her feet.

Now half the sky was black as doom, almost as dark as night,
as round the bend to Froggy's pond she stopped with pure delight,
for there before her nut-brown eyes, afloat in flowery-pot,
was Melody with aunty May, sailing to where knows what!

And as they spied Miss Twizzy there, they quickly rowed to shore,
to pull Miss Twizzy, 'all aboard' to sail and laugh some more.
While Froggy croaked to see such fun the mallards filled with dread,
and crayfish rose up from the depths, to see commotion spread.

The water sploshed and splished and splashed, the bamboos clicked a tune,
as swans with cygnets danced along, beside the old pontoon,
While nearer came the willow trees to whisper, drooping low,
for granma Otter from the bank, was waving on tiptoe.

Three damselflies upon the pond, gathered to stir a breeze,
to set the teapot on a course to view the pleasantries.
The little teapot with her crew cast headlong, free to roam
until aunt May declared, 'enough, we should be heading home.'

The day had been a great success, but dark now at twilight,
and Twizzy had a field of corn to navigate that night.
The stars were kind, so guided her home safely to her bed,
where dreams of such a cruise that day, packed full her little head.

Getting Fit

Miss Twizzy needs to exercise,
to eat less cheese and aunt May's fries,
so into Froggy's pond she'll swim
to stretch and tone each furry limb.

She's neither young nor very old
but knows her weight must be controlled,
to be as slender as can be -
with less to eat at lunch and tea.

She walks the paddock with a sigh
with two acorns she lifts chest high,
then runs where beans and carrots grow
avoiding farmer Squidge's hoe!

With heavy weights she tries her best
but Sissy swan seems unimpressed,
when Twizzy trips and with a cry
falls headlong into Percy's sty!

Then boxing with her own shadow
she lunges like a dynamo,
just missing Lily lamb's black nose
and Suzy piglet's dirty toes.

And yet she tries with dignity,
to shed her weight with sanity,
before she's portly like the cat,
for that would be the end of that!

But if she gets herself in shape
she'll leave that portly cat agape,
because with muscles built anew,
She won't be on his cat menu!!

The Cheesey Feast

One day when Mrs Squidge was out with only Twizzy there,
she climbed the tablecloth of check and sat atop to stare!
For there before her very eyes upon the tableware,
beside the teapot blue as sky, were crackers with cheese fare.

For Twizzy mouse there was too much, oh, far too much to eat,
beneath white daisies in the pot (I think called Marguerite)
and speaking to herself she said, 'now if I am discreet,
I'll nibble here and then from there to give myself a treat.'

She chomped on brie and wensleydale and then on shropshire blue,
on stilton and a cornish yarg, in fact, enough for two!
Then feeling rather over full, so full she couldn't chew,
she sat and watched her tummy grow, with whiskers bent askew!!

'Twas then she heard the portly cat, awaken from his nap
on hearing Mrs Squidge with screams, call for the new mouse-trap,
while chasing him around the yard, with broom for his mishap,
at letting Twizzy eat fine cheese, without leaving a scrap!

So poor MissTwizzy ran as fast as Geraldine the hare,
to wait, nursing her aching tum below the bottom stair,
but Mrs Squidge was angry and Miss Twizzy well aware
that portly cat was wrongly blamed, for cheese no longer there!!!

Miss Twizzy Says, 'No'

Miss Twizzy mouse is quite a catch, with nut-brown eyes and fur to match,
and every day she sings a song about young love the whole day long.
While her admirers I've been told, all faint and swoon quite uncontrolled,
with love songs ringing in their ears, they swing from drapes and chandeliers.
With starry eyes and smiles agape they come in all sizes and shape,
but Twizzy takes not hide nor hair of suitors she can hardly bear!
They come in droves with spring bouquets and gift wrapped cheese for her souffles',
while some come from the town in hats, in fancy ties and fancy spats,
you might deduce from those last words, that Twizzy mouse likes bees and birds
but sadly she is very shy and seeks instead to clarify,
that as a spinster she is thrilled, to live alone at which she's skilled.
So one by one the suitors leave, unloved and sad while some will grieve,
to leave Miss Twizzy at the farm with portly cat to cause alarm,
annoying farmer Squidge as well, arousing him with each nerve cell,
and in the kitchen Mrs Squidge, while baking pies will wreak carnage,
for if she sees Miss Twizzy there her rolling pin will fly through air,
so making Twizzy fast escape, before her head becomes misshape!
Some beaus' promise they will protect, to keep her safe
from harm direct, and wage a war with portly cat with machine fire –
Rat-a-ta-tat!!!!!

But Twizzy likes to be alone, no need for spouse or chaperone,
and so she closed her door and locked her suitors out who once had knocked!

Tangerine Treat

When Twizzy finds a tangerine
she peels it with great care,
for it's a treat not often seen
to her that can compare.

Last week she found a pineapple,
which took her days to peel,
her paws were tender, red and sore
its skin was hard as steel.

A raspberry, she'll eat that's ripe
or grapes gleaming with shine,
that fell upon the patio
from farmer Squidge's vine.

Bananas give her hic-hiccups
while grapefruits are too sour
and give her painful tummy aches
which seem to last an hour!

Should Mrs Squidge bake apple-pies
Miss Twizzy always knows,
where cores and peelings can be found
before they de-compose.

But Twizzy has a tangerine
today and it's her quest,
to peel it, taking extra care
to savour all the zest.

Harvest ...

'Twas early hours one misty morn with shadows faintly dark,
before the moon could wave, 'goodbye,' and long before the lark
caught in his beak a slith'ry worm upon the dew-kissed lawn,
when Farmer Squidge decided it was time to harvest corn.

His tractor woke Miss Twizzy as it hurtled past her door,
with hoots and shakey-shudderings, that shook her bedroom floor -
amusing Tilly spider on the picture, now askew
and woke the cock'rel Charlie from his roost, to 'cockle-doo.'

'The silks of corn now brown and dry are higher than a kite,'
squealed Twizzy Mouse to Melody as dawn broke ever bright,
while Farmer Squidge looked to the sky now turning turquoise blue,
instructing corn be gathered in, without further ado.

Along with cousin Melody, Miss Twizzy scampered past
the cows ready for milking and the bull, with eyes downcast,
while geese snake-headed lazily and rose up ever high -
all honking and a hollerin' across the morning sky.

They waited patiently all day until the corn was picked,
then piled inside the old store barn with keys that double-clicked.
'til on the stroke of midnight with the farm all fast asleep,
along with cousin Melody, Miss Twizzy took a peep.

Beneath the door they scampered in, and to their great delight
saw mountains of the sweetest corn just begging for a bite!
'Old Farmer Squidge won't mind I'm sure,' cried Twizzy, tremblin' fear
that portly cat would stir and wake, instead of snoring clear.

Both mice ate heartedly for hours 'til they could eat no more,
'til Farmer Squidge discovered them and bellowed with a roar -
while giving chase across the yard as Percy's piglets squealed,
and Melody and Twizzy fled across the new ploughed field.

Twizzy's Pinafore

Though scarce five minutes have since passed, or maybe ten or more,
since Twizzy could remember where she'd put her pinafore,
it wasn't where she thought it was nor was it in her drawer,
nor hanging on the pantry hook, nor lying on the floor.

'Where can it be,' she cried aloud to Tilly spider who,
was far too busy spinning webs for flies to rendezvous,
but Twizzy now was in a tizz, not knowing what to do
when suddenly she heard Brown owl, calling, 'tu-whit tu-whoo.'

'Tu-whit tu-whoo' he called again 'til Twizzy stepped outside
to see Brown owl all feathers fluffed, annoyed and bossy-eyed,
to say, while drifting on the breeze, becoming mystified
he'd seen Miss Twizzy's pinafore and Tommy thrush collide.

The wind had blown the pinafore off Twizzy's washing line,
Across the field to bluebell wood beside the old tin-mine,
As far as cousin Melody's and Froggy's 'fishing' sign,
Yet further still and back again, from four o'clock to nine!

The Leopard

Twizzy was bored without a clue as to the why's or what's,
or even the wherefore art thou's, or yet, the diddlysquat's!!
With that in mind she took a stroll and came across a zoo,
with lions and orang-utans, giraffe and kangaroo.

Hyenas laughed to see her there and monkeys thought, 'how brave,'
to see a little mouse walk by with giggles and a wave,
then elephants with feet like plates just missed her by an inch,
while beetles black as ebony smiled from their labyrinth.

A bear was dozing in the sun to scratch his itchy nose,
as Twizzy squealed, 'excuse me sir, I don't mean to impose.'
'Twas then she saw beyond the rail a piece of juicy meat,
so making Twizzy's whiskers twitch at such a scrummy treat.

She blinked with joy at her first taste of meat, but then, oh dear,
for suddenly she heard a growl, that shook the ground with fear,
A leopard in a coat of spots was bending over her,
Thus making Twizzy tremble more with each and ev'ry grrrrrrrrrrr!!!

'I've never seen a mouse before, would you be good to eat?'
'Oh no!' Cried Twizzy in despair now trying to retreat,
'well, in that case we shall be friends and I will share my food,
I'm sorry if I scared you dear, I don't mean to be rude.'

And so they ate a feast for kings and Mr Leopard purred,
'why don't you move in here to live, or is that too absurd?'
Miss Twizzy thought most carefully then looked him in the eye,
and squeaked a tremblin' 'no, kind sir,' but promised him a pie.

She peeled the apples all next day whilst no-one was about,
and with them baked a pie with pride of that she had no doubt,
and Mr Leopard ate the lot then gave Twizzy a kiss,
so making her blush scarlet red, there in the morning mist.

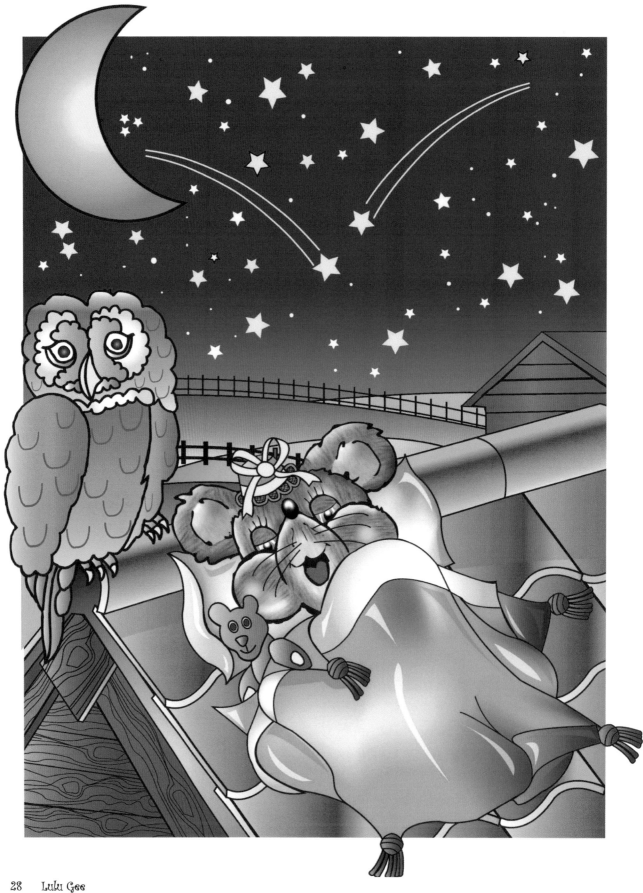

Sleeping Out ....

Miss Twizzy loves to go to bed but when too warm at night,
she clambers to the pitch tiled roof to sleep below moonlight,
for when the sky's darker than ink the stars shine there as well,
with trailing strands of silv'ryness, cross fields and primrose dell.

Brown owl plays hide and seek sometimes above her make-shift bed,
that's when she hides beneath her sheet to dream of cheese instead,
she plans always to stay awake, with so much night to see,
with so much in her part of sky how grand the rest must be.

Last night she tried to stay awake but soon forgot, and then -
heard Charlie cock'rel, 'cock-a-doo,' and it was day again!

When Twizzy Lost Her Voice

Miss Twizzy lost her voice today, by accident she thinks,
between a cough, two sneezing fits one hiccup and four blinks.
Her voice was lost, it wouldn't sing no matter how she tried,
so what to do now for the best she couldn't quite decide.

Perhaps it floated on the breeze, she trembled with dismay,
or hopped with Geraldine the hare 'cross meadow lands to play,
or singing loud in chorus rhyme with Milly nightingale,
or had it flown to Froggie's pond to swim with Sydney snail?

She searched in ev'ry pot and pan above the larder store,
while Tilly spider now awake searched ev'ry inch of floor,
then high above the kitchen shelf, behind the jars of rice,
beside the slice of apple pie she searched, not once but twice!

From morning 'til the afternoon poor Twizzy searched in vain,
as drawers were emptied one by one then all put back again
but now her head was aching sore with tears not far away,
like Georgie Porgie, puddin'and pie, her voice had gone astray.

That is, 'til cousin Melody heard of poor Twizzy's plight
from Tilly, still fast rummaging the depth and breadth and height
around the farm's old nooks and cracks and Percy pig's new sty,
more flustered by the minute as the night was almost nigh.

I know how we can find your voice laughed Melody at last,
who held a jar of honeycomb as Twizzy looked aghast!
'Two spoonfuls straightaway Twizzy is all I think you'll need,
'tis sweet and fresh from Bertie bee so therefore guaranteed.

So Twizzy found her voice at last with help from Melody,
who promptly put the kettle on to make a pot of tea -
while Tilly curled within her web and swinging to and fro,
fell fast asleep scarce unaware of Twizzy's voice below!

The Circus

From Twizzy's window she can see far out beyond the yard
across the meadows to the pond where ducklings promenade,
beneath skies blue and clear and fine with not a hint of grey,
yet Twizzy feels a naughtiness will come to her this day.

She overheard the portly cat tell of a thing so strange,
a circus, that had come to town, he'd seen it at close range,
with animals as big as trees with stripes upon their fur
and necks that reach up to the sky with strange names like, Ben Hur!

So when the sun was high and warm and bright in Twizzy's eyes,
she scampered off into the town to see what all implies,
then suddenly her eyes grew wide as saucers 'neath a cup,
as clowns in fancy coloured suits were calling, 'come, roll up!'

Miss Twizzy heard a marching band that made her front paws tap,
led by a man in scarlet coat with braid around his cap,
while acrobats tumbled from high to rapturous applause,
in costumes that could rival those of monsters in Star Wars.

But meanwhile as Miss Twizzy stood in awe of the parade,
she felt herself scooped up aloft and to all was displayed,
upon the elephant's long trunk that swayed from side to side,
who thought it fun to give Twizzy a lovely, joyous ride.

They ambled most unhurriedly and with a dawdling pace,
the elephant with Twizzy mouse were quite a rare showcase
and as they sashayed with the band the crowd looked with delight,
as Twizzy mouse sat without fear with squeals from her great height.

Then suddenly the portly cat, 'meowed' as loud could be,
for he had seen Miss Twizzy mouse as high as an oak tree
and elephant, with fear of cats reared up so Twizzy fell,
then quickly and with paws of speed jumped on the carousel.

And as she dodged the horse's hooves painted in many hues,
this way and that and in-between old portly cat pursues -
'til Twizzy reached a hiding place beneath a bale of hay,
with memories of naughtiness, upon this summer's day!

Twizzy's Second Christmas

'Twas one past the midnight when Miss Twizzy Mouse
was woken by something elsewhere in the house,
she'd heard a commotion, a sound from the roof,
a strange stomping sound like a soft reindeer hoof.

'Please let it be Santa' she heard herself cry,
with tears of excitement she couldn't deny,
before she could count past two, three and four
she felt Santa placing a gift in each paw.

A rosy-red apple with nibbles of cheese,
apricot nougat and warm dungarees -
to wear when escaping the old portly cat
and to keep ears cosy, a red velvet hat.

'Twas two past the midnight, now Santa was gone
as snow started falling and everywhere shone,
while all round the house there was nothing astir,
except for the rumble of portly cat's purr....Shhhhh!

Author's Biography:

Lulu Gee lives on the south coast of England, she worked in corporate finance until she retired and now writes full-time with her two dogs Teddy and Dolly never far from her side.

Her two previous books written in collaboration with the poet, Daniel Lake, have been extremely well received and she has a fast growing following of her work from the many poetry recitals she gives.

Her love of fantasy and the natural world has long inspired Lulu and through this genre she hopes to encourage a younger generation to appreciate poetry.

She was delighted to be made an honorary director of the International Poetry Fellowship (IPF) in 2013 and the same year won the much coveted Vera Rich memorial prize for her much acclaimed poem, 'Cumbria'.